EXPLORING MUSIC

Keyboards

and Electronic Music

Alyn Shipton

RSVP
RAINTREE
STECK-VAUGHN
P U B L I S H E R S
The Steck-Vaughn Company

Austin, Texas

Titles in the Series
Brass
Keyboards and Electronic Music
Percussion
Singing
Strings
Woodwinds

Editor: Pauline Tait
Picture research: Diana Morris
Design: Julian Holland
Illustrator: Terry Hadler
Electronic Production: Scott Melcer

Picture acknowledgments
The author and publishers wish to thank the following photographic sources: Barnaby's Picture Library: title page; Bridgeman Art Library: p7, p9 (bottom), p11, p17 (bottom), p21 (bottom); Robert Harding Picture Library: p6, p25 (top); Image Bank: p22; Jarrold Publishing: p20; Performing Arts Library: p5, p12, p14 (top), p28, p29; Redferns: p23, p26.

Cover credits
(Harry Connick Jr.) © Larry Busacca/Retna.

Library of Congress Cataloging-in-Publication Data

Shipton, Alyn.
    Keyboards and electronic music / Alyn Shipton.
      p.   cm. — (Exploring music)
    Includes index.
    Summary: Text and pictures introduce the keyboard family of instruments, such as harpsichords, pianos, organs, electronic organs, electronic keyboards, and electronic music. The role of conductor is also discussed.
    ISBN 0-8114-2318-2
    1. Keyboard instruments — Juvenile literature.   I. Title.
II. Series: Shipton, Alyn. Exploring music.
ML549.S5   1994
786'.19—dc20

                                  93-16637
                                        CIP
                                   AC MN

Printed and bound in the United States
1 2 3 4 5 6 7 8 9 0 VH 99 98 97 96 95 94 93

Contents

What Is a Keyboard Instrument?

Musical instruments are normally grouped according to how they make their sound. String instruments have strings that vibrate, woodwind instruments have reeds that vibrate, and percussion instruments are struck or hit to make them vibrate.

Keyboard instruments are not grouped by how they make their sound. All three methods of sound production—strings, reeds, and percussion—are found in these instruments. Instead, keyboard instruments are a family of instruments that are all operated the same way. They have a mechanism that allows just one player to make a whole range of notes, and to play several notes at the same time. The keyboard is a series of levers or switches, each of which operates a different note.

Sound

When any object vibrates, it makes a sound. Its vibrations are carried through the air in waves called sound waves. We can identify the sounds made by different objects because no two things vibrate in exactly the same way, and so no two things make exactly the same pattern of sound waves.

The main points that help us to identify a particular sound are:

volume: how loud it is,
pitch: how high or low it is, and
tone: the quality of the sound.

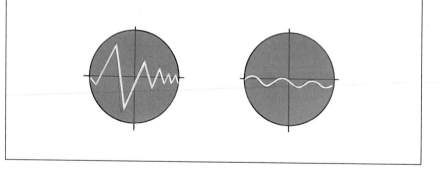

These oscilloscope pictures show the patterns of sound waves. On the left is the jagged pattern of noise made by an untuned instrument. On the right is the even pattern of a note played by a tuned musical instrument.

WHAT DOES A KEYBOARD LOOK LIKE?

An organ called a *hydraulis* was invented in 250 B.C. in Greece. It had a small number of pipes, and one lever to operate each one. In the Middle Ages, organs still had large and simple keyboards, with levers or **sliders** operating single notes, or sometimes two or three notes together.

Because organs had only a few large **keys**, they could not be played quickly, or produce more than one note at a time. So, between 1300 and 1400 the modern keyboard was gradually developed, with the familiar arrangement of black and white keys. Each key was only a little wider than the player's finger.

This organ from the time of Handel (1685–1759) has a single keyboard. Like many organs of its time, the black and white keys are reversed: The main notes are black, and the sharps and flats are white.

The range of notes a keyboard can operate from bottom to top is called its **compass**. The notes themselves are grouped in **octaves**. Each octave has eight "white" keys, and five "black" keys. The white notes are the eight notes of the C-major **scale**. The black notes are **semitones**, or half-notes, that fall between the main notes of this scale.

Some inventors have tried to make more complex keyboards that operate more notes or play some of the sounds that fall between the notes of the scale. Few of these have ever been popular.

The standard piano keyboard with the normal arrangement of "white" and "black" keys

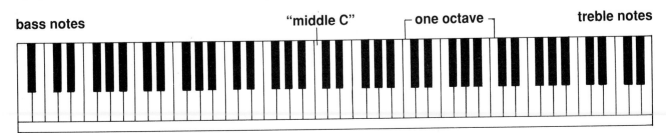

bass notes   "middle C"   ⌐ one octave ⌐   treble notes

How Keyboard Instruments Work

There are three main kinds of keyboard instruments:
1. those that make their sound by hitting or plucking strings,
2. those that make their sound by blowing air into a pipe or past a reed, and
3. electronic keyboards.

STRINGS

The principle on which string keyboard instruments work involves strings that are tightly stretched across a frame, with each string tuned to a different note. Many instruments, like the piano and harpsichord, have groups of strings tuned to each individual note of the scale. When each string is hit with a hammer or a **tangent**, or is plucked with a **jack**, it makes a sound.

Keyboard instruments with strings fall into two groups:
1. those on which the string is hit—the clavichord, fortepiano, and piano, and
2. those on which the string is plucked—the harpsichord, spinet, and virginal.

The largest of the plucked string keyboard instruments is the harpsichord. This concert instrument was used by the composer Haydn (1732–1809).

PIPES AND REEDS

Keyboard instruments with pipes and reeds are generally known as organs. There is usually an air pump somewhere in the instrument that forces air into the pipes or past the reeds. The keyboard switches the air supply and directs it into particular pipes or past reeds to make individual notes.

Small, portable organs have only one set of pipes or reeds, but big concert hall or church organs have many sets, or **ranks**, of pipes.

This church organ is in the Piccadilly area in London and was built in the 1600s. It has several ranks of pipes, and they are in a case with sculptures by the carver Grinling Gibbons. Many organs from the 1600s and 1700s have similar decorations.

ELECTRONIC KEYBOARDS

Electronic keyboards look like ordinary piano or organ keyboards, but they make their sound entirely through the use of electronics. They were developed from electric organs and from a variety of experimental electric instruments. Now many families have an electronic piano that takes up less space than an ordinary one and never goes out of tune. When it is attached to a **synthesizer**, an electronic keyboard can produce many of the sounds of the orchestra. If it is hooked up to a personal computer it can be used for a whole range of musical tasks, from printing out notes to composing electronic music.

To make a sound, an electronic keyboard has to be played through loudspeakers—it makes no sound of its own. Some musicians find it very convenient to practice on a keyboard with headphones.

The Harpsichord Family

Harpsichords, spinets, and virginals all work in the same way. Each key is a lever that pushes a jack up past the string when the player presses the key down. The jack is not connected to the key, and gravity makes it fall back. On its upward journey, a piece of quill sticking out of the jack at an angle plucks the string. As the jack falls back, the quill flips out of the way of the string, and does not pluck the note again. The different instruments of the family are identified by their shape.

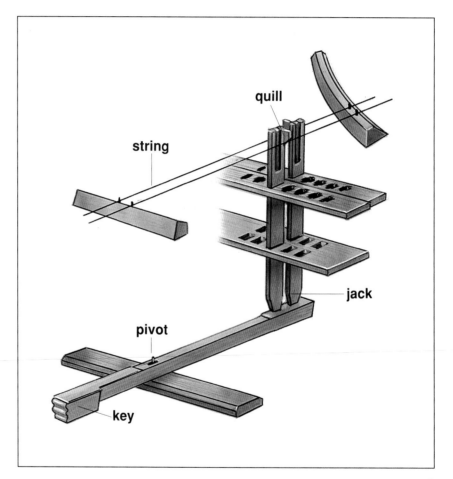

The "action" of a harpsichord showing how the key operates the jack

THE VIRGINAL

The virginal is the simplest of this group of instruments. Its strings are in a big rectangular box, and they run across from left to right in front of the player. The keyboard is set into the long side of the box, slightly to the left of center.

Virginals have one string for each note, and one jack for each string. The instrument was popular in the 16th century. Some unusual virginals have a second keyboard, with its own soundbox and strings, that sits above the main instrument. A "mother and child" double virginal like this allows the player to introduce more variety into the music. The upper keyboard can be played by itself, or together with the lower one, which operates both sets of jacks.

THE SPINET

Spinets have their strings set at a diagonal from the keyboard. Their cases look like big wedges of cheese. Inside the lid, there are often paintings of landscapes or imaginary scenes.

A 17th century "octave" spinet

THE HARPSICHORD

Harpsichords look something like slender grand pianos, but they often have two keyboards and several sets of strings. The harpsichord was invented in the early 1500s and was designed to do many more things than the spinet. Different sets of strings can be played together, and contrasts are made by using one hand on each keyboard, or **manual**. One manual operates one set of strings, the second operates another.

An 18th century French chamber concert with musicians and listeners grouped around the harpsichord

Listening Guide
Harpsichords were used for all manner of music, from **solo** playing to **ensembles**. They frequently played the rhythmic **continuo** parts that accompanied orchestral pieces and operas. For solo music, listen to Domenico Scarlatti's many hundred sonatas, Johann Sebastian Bach's *Italian Concerto*, and the many pieces by François Couperin. Bach also wrote concertos for harpsichord and strings. Great players include Christopher Hogwood, George Malcolm, and, in the early 20th century, Wanda Landowska.

Tangents and Hammers

The mechanism of this 16th century clavichord includes curved hammers that align with the bass strings.

THE CLAVICHORD

The clavichord is one of the quietest and smallest of keyboard instruments. It looks similar to the virginal, with a rectangular case and a keyboard set into the long side. Its sound is produced by brass blades called tangents hitting the strings. These tangents are at the opposite end of each key from the player's finger. When the key is pressed down, the tangent strikes the string. Different notes are produced depending on the length of string between the tangent and the bridge of the instrument.

The first clavichords had many keys, but only a few strings. Different keys made different lengths of a string vibrate, and so one string could produce a range of notes. This kind of clavichord could not be used to play chords of several notes together, so new clavichords were designed with a string for each note. A skilled player can vary the pressure on the key, and create a **vibrato**, as the tangent touches the string.

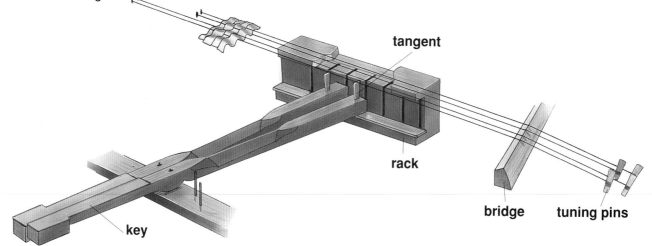

tangent

rack

bridge   tuning pins

key

A close-up of the clavichord mechanism. The length of string between the tangent and the bridge vibrates to make each note. The tuning pins adjust the tension of the string.

Clavichord Playing

If you have had some piano lessons, you will know the basic skills of keyboard playing. If you then change to the clavichord you will learn how to get the most out of this quiet instrument and the music written for it in the 18th century by C.P.E. Bach. The clavichord is too quiet for most chamber groups and can only be played as a solo instrument in peaceful, intimate surroundings where it can be heard easily. Some composers wrote special music for it, including Neefe, Türk, and Rust.

THE FORTEPIANO

The piano makes a sound when its strings are hit by **hammers**. The first piano was built by Bartolomeo Cristofori in 1698. It looked like a harpsichord in shape, and he called it a "harpsichord with loud and soft." The Italian words for loud and soft are "forte" and "piano" and these gave the instrument its name. Today, we call the instruments of the 18th and early 19th centuries "fortepianos" to distinguish them from the modern "pianoforte," which is the full name of the piano.

This fortepiano was built in 1775. It has a rectangular case like a harpsichord, without the smooth curves of the modern grand piano.

Modern Pianos

Pianos these days come in three basic shapes: the grand piano, the square piano, and the upright piano. In the first two types, the hammers move upward to hit strings that are arranged horizontally. In the upright piano the strings are vertical, and the hammers are arranged in front of them, moving forward to hit the strings.

THE GRAND PIANO

The concert grand piano is a direct descendant of the instruments built by Cristofori. Its strings stretch away from the player at right angles to the keyboard, and the case is over six feet (two meters) long. The keys operate the hammers by means of an **action**—a system of levers and springs very much like the one invented by Cristofori. They are designed so that the hammer will not bounce up again and hit the string a second time. To make the case smaller, and more manageable for the average house, "baby," or "mini" grand pianos are built with "overstrung" strings. In these pianos the longest strings are laid diagonally across the frame, and across the other strings, to save length.

A small modern grand piano. It is "overstrung," and the bass strings (on the left) are placed over the middle register strings to save space. The frame is metal and designed to take high tension strings that will produce loud notes and a strong tone.

THE SQUARE PIANO

The square piano is not really square. It looks something like a virginal, but with a bigger keyboard. The strings are stretched from left to right in the frame, so it is more compact than the grand piano. It was a popular instrument in homes in Europe and the United States at the end of the 18th century. The English writer Jane Austen had one in her drawing room on which she and her family and friends played.

THE UPRIGHT PIANO

These days most houses that have a piano have an upright instrument. This type of piano was invented in the 19th century, and the strings are stretched in a vertical case. If you take the front off an upright piano, you can see the mechanism. It consists of rows of hammers that move away from the player, hitting the strings at about the player's eye level.

PIANO PEDALS

All pianos have at least two pedals. The one on the right is the **sustaining pedal**. The sustaining pedal lifts the piano's felt **dampers** away from the strings, allowing notes to sound for a long (or "sustained") time. The pedal on the left is the **soft pedal**, intended to make the sounds quieter. It moves the hammers of a grand piano so that they only hit two of the three strings of each note. On an upright piano, this pedal operates an additional felt damper.

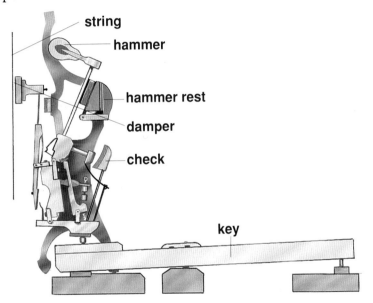

Today's upright pianos have a complex mechanism designed to fit in a small space. This diagram shows the major components that operate each note.

The Player Piano

Pianos were popular for home entertainment in the late 1800s and early 1900s. In the era before radio and television, with sound recording in its early stages, families made their own music. Inventors, realizing that there would be a market for mechanical or automatic pianos, invented the pianola, or "player piano." The pianola used a roll of paper with holes punched in it for each note. Air was sucked through the holes, and worked the hammers of the piano. At first, someone had to pump the air with foot pedals, but later electric pumps were used. Rolls cut by great players like Debussy and Mahler show us how they sounded in the days before it was possible to make records.

Prepared and Modified Pianos

John Cage (1912–1992)

Some of the objects used to make a "prepared piano" include nails and bolts.

The name "prepared" piano was first used by the American composer John Cage in 1940. He carefully placed bolts, screws, rubber erasers, and other objects between the strings of a grand piano. When the notes were played, many of them took on new and different sounds, including odd buzzes and twangs. Other composers, like Henry Cowell, discovered the range of sounds that could be made using the inside of the piano, and by plucking or stroking the strings with the hands instead of using the keys and hammers. Some of Cowell's pieces, like The Banshee and Sinister Resonance, produce strange music that does not sound like normal piano playing at all.

Piano Playing

The piano is one of the most rewarding instruments to learn to play. It has a vast range of music written for it, from all periods and at all levels of difficulty. The first things you will learn are how to read two lines of music at once (one for each hand), and how to coordinate both hands at the keys. The piano can prepare you to play all the other keyboard instruments in this book. It will also allow you to make music with other people, as an accompanist to soloists and singers, or in instrumental groups.

Listening Guide

Many composers have written for solo pianists. The sonatas by Mozart, Haydn, and Beethoven have been recorded by many great soloists. Listen to recordings of these by historical figures like Arthur Rubinstein and Vladimir Horowitz, or more modern recordings by Alfred Brendel, Maurizio Pollini, and Daniel Barenboim. Other words for solo piano include Chopin's mazurkas and polonaises, Liszt's rhapsodies, and Debussy's impressionistic pieces.

There are many concertos for piano and orchestra. Some composers, like Rachmaninoff and Gershwin, made records of their own compositions. Other concertos, by Mozart, Beethoven, Tchaikovsky, and Grieg have been recorded by many pianists. Some great conductors who have also played the piano, such as Leonard Bernstein and André Previn, have recorded Mozart's concertos.

Jazz pianists have developed great skill and speed at the piano. Try to hear records by Art Tatum, Fats Waller, Earl Hines, and Teddy Wilson. The Canadian pianist Oscar Peterson trained as a classical player but played jazz for most of his long career. He plays with dazzling dexterity, both on his own and with a trio (of bass and drums, or bass and guitar).

Reed Organs

One of the earliest and simplest types of organs is made of a keyboard joined to a set of **free reeds**, like those of a mouth organ, with a pair of bellows to pump air through the reeds automatically.

Organs like this do not have pipes, and their reeds take up relatively little space, so they are very compact instruments. Since the early 16th century most portable organs have had some kind of reed to make their sound.

REGALS

The name given to a commonly used type of reed organ in the early 16th century was the regal. Two people operated the instrument, one playing the keys and the other pumping two large bellows from a position facing the player. Air from the bellows was forced through a **pallet** to operate a reed when each key was pressed down by the player.

One curious type of regal, built by an instrument maker named Voll in Nuremberg, had bellows designed to look like huge leather-bound books. When not in use, the whole instrument folded up to look like a leather Bible. Such instruments are called "Bible regals." If you had gone to an English pageant or play in the 16th century, the music would probably have been played on regals.

Two players show how a regal was operated and how these little reed organs were designed to be portable.

HARMONIUM

The harmonium is a kind of reed organ, invented in 1842, and first made by the French builder A.F. Debain. At first, harmoniums had just one set of reeds and one key for each reed. Later, more sets of reeds were added, and sliding levers called **stops** were built into the casing above the keys to allow the player to select different groups of reeds. When the stop was pulled out, that set of reeds would be operated.

Harmonium players have to pump air into the instrument themselves, using their feet. As the player's feet pump up and down, he or she can also control the volume of the instrument with the knees, using flaps that swing forward underneath the keyboard. As the player swings the knees apart, pressing on the flaps, the sound of the instrument gets louder.

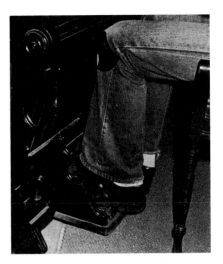

A player operates the foot pedals to pump air into a harmonium. The flap that controls volume is visible beside the player's left knee.

A 19th-century reed organ complete with an elaborate mahogany case

Listening Guide

In the 19th century, a lot of music was written for the reed organ by the French composers Louis Vierne and César Franck, who also taught the instrument. Some records of their work have been made, although much of it is played on the church or concert organ instead. Kurt Weill wrote music for the reed organ to accompany songs in his *Threepenny Opera*.

The Organ

Full-sized organs are giant instruments that can usually be found in churches, concert halls, and theaters. They are so large that they have to be built into position, but even though they are so big they work in much the same way as the small reed organs. The main differences are that the sound is made by pipes rather than only by reeds, and that everything is on a larger scale.

The main parts of an organ are a **wind chest**, which is pumped full of air by bellows or by an electric pump, the keyboards (which operate pallets to direct the air to the pipes), and the pipes themselves.

BELLOWS AND WIND CHESTS

In the ancient Greek instrument with pipes and a wind chest, called the *hydraulis* (see page 4), air was pumped into a central cavity and was kept under pressure by a tank of water. The water held down valves to allow air in but not out, so it forced air through to the organ pipes. By the 11th century, organs had been built in many churches. For 800 years they were pumped by hand, one person pumping as another played, until the invention of electric bellows and air pumps.

This is a cross section of an 18th century French organ. It shows how air from the bellows enters the wind chest and is released into the pipes by levers operated from the keyboard.

KEYBOARDS

If you look at most church or theater organs, you will see that they have two or more keyboards. If you look down at the player's feet, there will be another keyboard—a set of pedals designed to be played with the feet. Each keyboard or manual operates a different group (or rank) of pipes. These can be played together by using the **couplers** that link the keyboards to one another. A skilled organist will be capable of playing on two keyboards and the pedalboard at the same time, as well as quickly pulling out the stops that control each set of pipes. When all the pipes are in use together, the sound is very loud and is called "full organ."

The five manuals of the organ in St. Paul's Cathedral, London

PIPES

Most organs have three types of pipes. They are called **flue pipes**, **reed pipes**, and free reeds. Flue pipes are like recorders and flutes in the woodwind family. The air is split by a lip or sharp edge, and this makes the sound. Reed pipes are sort of like saxophones. They have a "shallot," which is somewhat like the mouthpiece of a saxophone. A brass reed vibrates against it as air is blown through the pipe. Free reeds are just like those in a harmonica or in a reed organ, attached to a pipe. The length and width of a pipe controls the note it makes.

In the diagram below, (a) and (b) show how a flue pipe works. Air enters at the pipe foot and is split by the flue. Pipes (c) and (d) are shown on their sides. Reed pipes, like (c), have their reed and shallot placed in the "boot" of the pipe. A free reed, like (d), is cut out of a narrow brass plate.

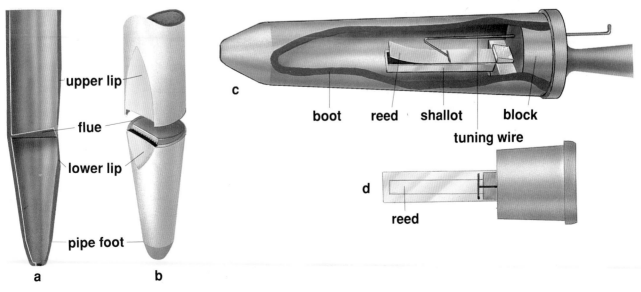

LOUD AND SOFT

Unlike the piano, which was designed to be louder or softer according to how hard the keys are pressed down, most organs do not have keys that work in this way. Because the keys are valves, opening and shutting pipes, a sound is made for as long as the key is pressed down and the valve is held open. An organ gets louder when you add more pipes by pulling out more stops. It gets quieter when you close off some of the pipes. One device that controls the volume of an organ is called a **swell box**. It consists of a large chamber with shutters that open and close. Inside the chamber is a set of pipes. Using a pedal, the organist can open or close the shutters. The sound from the pipes gets louder or softer according to how far the shutters are open.

Modern designers have incorporated swell boxes into the appearance of their instruments. One of the most spectacular swell boxes is in New College Chapel at Oxford University in England, where the shutters are glass. They catch the patterns of the surrounding stained glass as they open and shut, reflecting dramatic patterns of light.

New College Chapel at Oxford University in England

Organ Playing

If you want to learn the organ, it is a good idea to start with the piano and learn how to control your hands, because once you start the organ you'll need to train your feet to operate pedals as well! Many churches, concert halls, and theaters have organs that you can make an appointment to inspect.

Listening Guide

Some of the world's finest organ music dates from the early 18th century, with the compositions of J.S. Bach, Dietrich Buxtehude, and G.F. Handel. Many of their pieces have been recorded by E. Power Biggs and Virgil Fox. In the 19th century, with the invention of larger organs with many more pipes and tones, Widor, Saint-Saëns, and Liszt were able to write music in a very different and romantic style. Saint-Saëns wrote three organ "fantasies" and Widor wrote organ "symphonies" in which both composers treated the organ like an orchestra. In the 1900s, composers realized that there were large and impressive sounds that could only be made on the organ. The French composer Olivier Messiaen was one of the most imaginative and original composers for the organ in pieces like his *Meditations*.

Liszt and Wagner

Electronic Organs

Full-sized organs cannot easily be moved from the places in which they are built. Although reed organs are mobile, they do not have the range of sound or volume of a full-sized instrument. Musicians wanted a portable instrument with much of the character and range of the full organ. To solve their problem, the American engineer Laurens Hammond developed an organ that used electronics to produce its sound.

Hammond's first instruments appeared in 1935. A Hammond organ looks something like a small upright piano. It has two keyboards, foot pedals, and a set of **drawbars** near the keys that control the tone of the organ. Inside the case is a set of revolving wheels, one for each note. Cut into each wheel is a wave pattern, and when the wheel turns near a magnet, it makes an electrical pattern that can be turned into sound through a loudspeaker.

Different types of electric organs were invented after Hammond's instrument appeared. These make their sounds using a variety of methods, although all of them need a loudspeaker for the sounds to be heard.

The kind of loudspeaker used by an organ affects its sound. One of the most unusual speakers is called the Leslie Speaker™. The whole inside of the loudspeaker rotates, and this produces a pleasant throbbing effect for listeners.

A Hammond organ, showing the drawbars between the music stand and the top manual

Electronic Organ Playing

Electric or electronic organs are very popular home instruments because they can make almost the same variety of sounds as a full-sized instrument, but they take only a little more space than a piano. You'll still need to learn the piano to get started, but once you've begun to play the organ you'll find there are many clubs for amateur organists. There is also a network of festivals and competitions for young organists, many of them sponsored by organ makers.

Jimmy Smith

Listening Guide

The first recordings made on the Hammond organ included jazz pieces by Fats Waller. As people followed his example, the instrument became very popular with jazz and blues players, as well as with soul musicians like Ray Charles and Billy Preston. Among the jazz players who made records on the Hammond organ are Jimmy Smith ("Midnight Special"), Jimmy McGriff ("Blues for Mr. Jimmy"), Groove Holmes ("Soul Message"), and Shirley Scott ("Great Scott!").

The tradition of using big theater or large hall organs to play popular hits is continued today by organists in places like Radio City Music Hall in New York City.

Electronic Keyboards

Electronic keyboards are a giant technical step forward from electronic organs. Using powerful microprocessors, they contain the sound of real instruments coded into their memories. If you want your electronic keyboard to sound like a flute, you can program it to produce sound waves through its loudspeaker that sound almost exactly like the real thing.

Composers can analyze the sound waves that each individual instrument makes. By producing a digital "map" of the sound, in particular what is called its "envelope," the computer can be programmed to produce a similar map and reproduce the original sound. The envelope of a sound is made up of three parts: the **attack**, sustain, and decay of a sound. In other words, it is how a sound starts, continues, and then dies away. No two instruments have the same envelope.

Digitizing the sound of instruments in this way is called "sampling." One portable sequencer, for example, can play samples of 30 melody instruments and 26 drum sounds. It can then put these into any sequence you choose, using an ordinary electronic keyboard to program in the notes you want to play. If you want to add a rhythm backing of your own, then the same instrument has 76 backing rhythms already in its memory for you to choose from. The keyboard simply tells the computer what music you would like it to play.

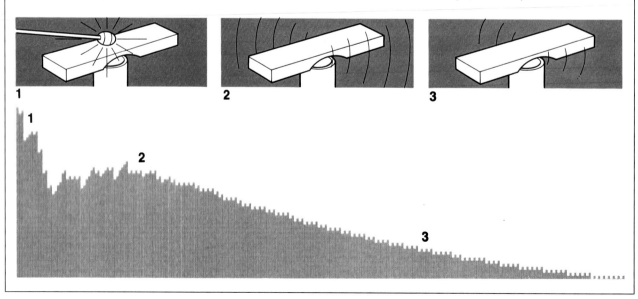

Attack: The note is begun by the sharp sound of a beater hitting the xylophone bar.

Sustain: As the note sounds, it reverberates and sustains.

Decay: As the note starts to die away, it reverberates less, decays, and stops.

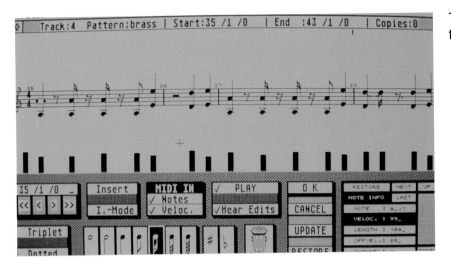

Typical music software produces this kind of screen display.

USING A PERSONAL COMPUTER

One kind of keyboard that only a few years ago nobody would have expected to be used for composing was the ordinary typewriter keyboard attached to a computer. When it is attached to a personal computer (PC) with music software, however, the keyboard is a powerful tool in helping composers write their own music and perform it electronically using their computer. You can get the **staff** to appear on the screen of your PC, using the typewriter keys to set up the **tempo**, rhythm, and so on. Then, using the mouse, you can start writing music right on the screen, which your computer will then play for you.

Composers use this technique when they are writing for different instruments, and they want to know quickly what their music is likely to sound like when it is performed by real instruments. Not only will the computer try it out for you, but when you are satisfied, you can print out the parts to give to a group of instrumentalists!

Effective use of a PC is enhanced by using an electronic music keyboard as well as the computer.

Electronic Music

Much of the music we hear on television or in film sound tracks is played entirely on synthesizers. This is the name given to electronic keyboards that reproduce the sounds of many other instruments. Synthesizers can also make sounds that no ordinary instrument could make, by using electronics to manufacture new sound patterns.

The German band Tangerine Dream performs their music entirely on synthesizers, with the members of the group using their keyboards to make a huge variety of sounds. Although they play in concert performances, the band does much of its work in the recording studio. This is where the synthesizer is most useful. One musician, working alone with a synthesizer and a multitrack tape recorder, can build up the sound of a whole orchestra.

Tangerine Dream

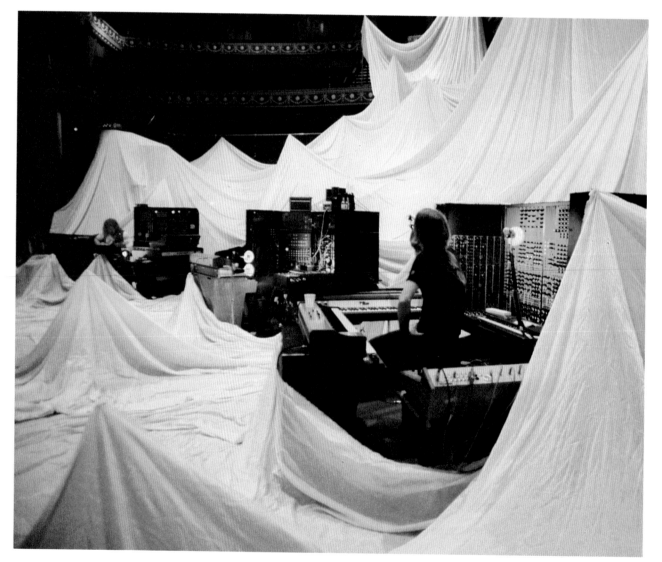

ELECTRONICS

Popular from the 1930s to the early 1950s, the theramin was among the earliest electronic instruments. A thin rod about 18 inches tall extended vertically from one end of an enclosure about the size of a small microwave oven. As the musician's hand approached or pulled back from this antenna, a musical tone rose or fell in pitch. After the introduction of analog tape recorders in 1947, several composers created new musical forms using tuned electronic oscillators and tape recorders. The 1956 film *Forbidden Planet* was the first to use music composed this way.

Electronic Music Playing
A music software package can probably be found for most home and school computers. This will allow you to compose on the screen, using the mouse, and to hear what you have written. You can also play electronic music on any keyboard that includes a synthesizer and a memory.

An electronic workshop

Listening Guide
There are many recordings of electronic music. Much that we hear on the radio everyday has electronic drums and rhythms, used as backing for rock and pop singers. Composers like Vangelis have produced whole film sound tracks electronically (like his music for *Blade Runner*). Thomas Dolby pioneered the recording of albums using electronic music. Tangerine Dream's music is on albums like *Melrose, Optical Race*, and *Lily on the Beach*. Players like Eddie Jobson have used music computers to create records. Other musicians who have created electronic film scores include the Greek composer Yanni and the pianist Suzanne Ciani.

Vangelis

27

The Conductor

Conductors may not seem to belong in a book about keyboard instruments, but the job of a conductor was originally performed by the orchestra's harpsichord player.

The small orchestras of the 17th and 18th centuries needed someone to make sure that all the musicians kept to the beat, came in at the right places, and obeyed the composer's instructions about how the music should be played. The harpsichordists took on the job of the conductor. They played the chords that accompanied singers or soloists, they often added extra notes to the ones being played by the other instruments, and they signaled to other players how to play their parts in a performance.

Eventually, the conductor emerged from behind the keyboard and took up a place in front of the orchestra, clearly visible to all musicians and to the audience. By the late 19th century, the role of a conductor was very much what it is today.

Vladimir Ashkenazy conducts an orchestra from the keyboard.

The conductor usually holds a white stick (or **baton**) in his or her right hand, for setting the time and signaling to the players what is expected of them. Some conductors do not use a baton but rely entirely on hand gestures.

THE CONDUCTOR'S JOB

The conductor is the person who decides how a composer's instructions are to be interpreted by an orchestra. In particular, the conductor decides:

how fast the piece is played,

how loud and soft it is to be, and

how the different instruments are to balance one another, and which ones are to be most prominent.

A conductor has to read and learn very thoroughly the music that the orchestra is to play. It is important that he or she be able to spot any tiny mistakes in the rehearsals and to correct them in time for a final performance.

Listening Guide

It is possible to learn a lot about the conductor's part in a performance by comparing different recordings. The same piece of music may last for 20 minutes on one recording, and only 18 minutes on another, depending on the tempo the conductor chooses. Some conductors highlight particular details, and make a few notes played by a clarinet or flute stand out. Listen to recordings conducted by Simon Rattle, Jane Glover, Sarah Caldwell, and Jeffrey Tate. In concertos, the conductor has to balance the orchestra and the solo instrument.

Simon Rattle

Glossary

action   the mechanism that produces a note from the strings or pipes of a keyboard instrument when a key is pressed

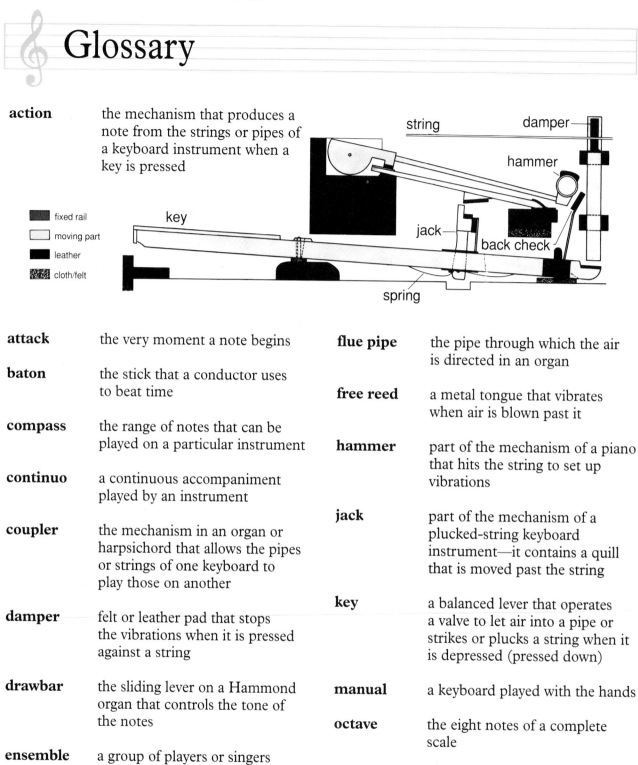

fixed rail
moving part
leather
cloth/felt

string   damper   hammer   key   jack   back check   spring

attack   the very moment a note begins

baton   the stick that a conductor uses to beat time

compass   the range of notes that can be played on a particular instrument

continuo   a continuous accompaniment played by an instrument

coupler   the mechanism in an organ or harpsichord that allows the pipes or strings of one keyboard to play those on another

damper   felt or leather pad that stops the vibrations when it is pressed against a string

drawbar   the sliding lever on a Hammond organ that controls the tone of the notes

ensemble   a group of players or singers

flue pipe   the pipe through which the air is directed in an organ

free reed   a metal tongue that vibrates when air is blown past it

hammer   part of the mechanism of a piano that hits the string to set up vibrations

jack   part of the mechanism of a plucked-string keyboard instrument—it contains a quill that is moved past the string

key   a balanced lever that operates a valve to let air into a pipe or strikes or plucks a string when it is depressed (pressed down)

manual   a keyboard played with the hands

octave   the eight notes of a complete scale

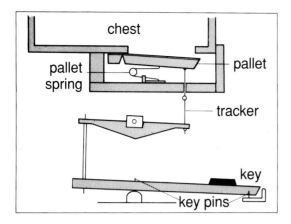

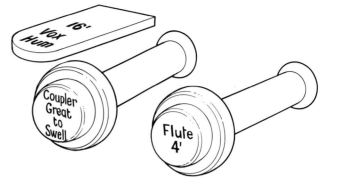

pallet   a valve

pitch   the level of a note, indicated by its position on the scale

rank   a complete set or row of pipes controlled by one stop in an organ

reed pipe   organ pipes in which the sound is made by a metal reed at the foot of the pipe

scale   a steplike, ordered arrangement of notes

semitone   half a tone; half step

slider   a valve that slides to open the air passage to an organ pipe

soft pedal   the pedal on a piano that either moves the keyboard so fewer strings are hit by the hammers, or places a felt damper on them to make the sound softer

solo   a passage played by one performer alone

sound wave   the movement of sound through the air, caused by a vibrating object

staff   the lines on which music notes are written

stop   a knob or button used to control sets of pipes in an organ (or the sets of pipes themselves)

sustaining pedal   the right-hand pedal on a piano which, when depressed, raises the dampers so that the strings can vibrate

swell box   the part of an organ in which pipes are enclosed, with shutters that open or close to control volume

synthesizer   an electronic instrument that can process and produce a wide variety of sounds

tangent   part of the mechanism in a clavichord that strikes the string

tempo   the quickness or speed with which a piece of music is played

tone   the quality of a sound

vibrato   a variation in the pitch of a note, repeated so rapidly that the note seems to stay the same, but with a "tremble"

volume   how loud a sound is

wind chest   the part of an organ that contains air under pressure so it can be fed to the pipes

Index

© 1993 Zoë Books Limited